Bob Seger for Ukulele

Page	Title	Page	Title
2	AGAINST THE WIND	40	OLD TIME ROCK & ROLL
6	BEAUTIFUL LOSER	43	RAMBLIN' GAMBLIN' MAN
14	BETTY LOU'S GETTIN' OUT TONIGHT	46	THE REAL LOVE
18	FEEL LIKE A NUMBER	52	ROLL ME AWAY
9	FIRE LAKE	49	STILL THE SAME
22	HOLLYWOOD NIGHTS	56	TILL IT SHINES
28	IN YOUR TIME	59	TURN THE PAGE
30	LIKE A ROCK	62	WAIT FOR ME
25	MAINSTREET	68	WE'VE GOT TONIGHT
34	NIGHT MOVES	65	YOU'LL ACCOMP'NY ME

Cover Photo © Michael Ochs Archives/Getty Images

ISBN 978-1-4803-9384-4

HAL•LEONARD®
CORPORATION
7777 W. BLUEMOUND RD. P.O. BOX 13819 MILWAUKEE, WI 53213

Visit Hal Leonard Online at
www.halleonard.com

Against the Wind

Words and Music by Bob Seger

First note

Verse
Moderate Rock beat

1. It seems like yes - ter - day, ___
2. *See additional lyrics*
3. *Instrumental*

but it was long a - go. ___

Ja - ney was love - ly. She was the queen of my nights, ___

there in the dark - ness with the ra - di - o play-in' low, ___ and

C

the se - crets that we shared, _____

Em

the moun - tains that we moved, _____

F   C

caught _ like a wild-fire out of con - trol _____ till there was

F   G

noth - in' left _ to burn _ and noth-in' left to prove. _

Pre-Chorus

Am   G

1. And I re - mem - ber what she _____ said to
2., 3. *See additional lyrics*

C   Am   F

me, _____ how she swore _____ that it nev - er would end. _

3

Outro

Well, I'm old - er now, ___ and still

run - nin'   a - gainst   the   wind,

Repeat and fade

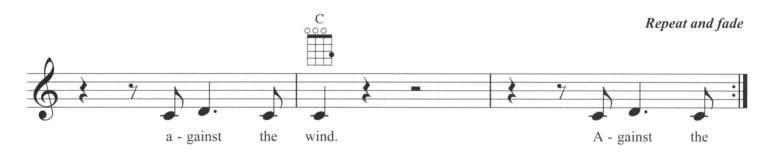

a - gainst   the   wind.   A - gainst   the

Additional Lyrics

2. And the years rolled slowly past,
   And I found myself alone,
   Surrounded by strangers I thought were my friends.
   I found myself further and further from my home,
   And I guess I lost my way.
   There were, oh, so many roads.
   I was livin' to run and runnin' to live,
   Never worried about payin', or even how much I owed.

Pre-Chorus: Movin' eight miles a minute for months at a time,
Breakin' all of the rules that would bend,
I began to find myself searchin',
Searchin' for shelter again and again.

Chorus: Against the wind,
Little somethin' against the wind.
I found myself seekin' shelter against the wind.

3. *Instrumental*

Pre-Chorus: Well, those drifter's days are past me now.
I've got so much more to think about:
Deadlines and commitments,
What to leave in, what to leave out.

Chorus: Against the wind,
I'm still runnin' against the wind.
I'm older now, but still runnin' against the wind.

Beautiful Loser

Words and Music by Bob Seger

1. He wants to dream like a young man
2. He's your old-est and your best friend;
3. *Instrumental*

with the wis-dom of an old man. He wants his home and se-
if you need him, he'll be there a-gain. ____ He's al-ways will-ing to be

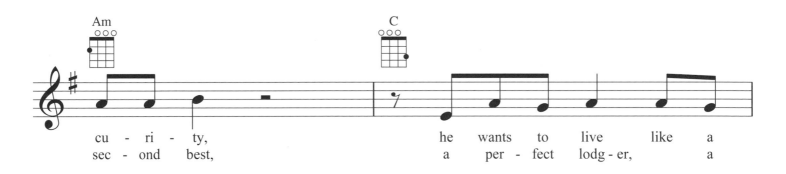

cu-ri-ty, he wants to live like a
sec-ond best, a per-fect lodg-er, a

Chorus

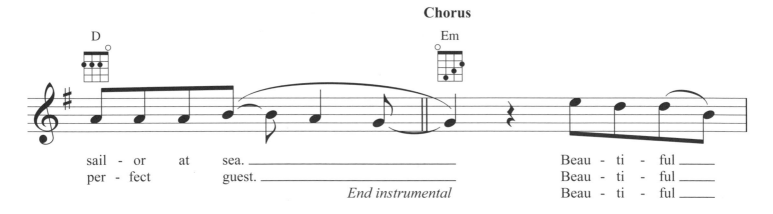

sail-or at sea. ____ Beau-ti-ful ____
per-fect guest. ____ Beau-ti-ful ____
End instrumental Beau-ti-ful ____

los - er, _____   where ___ you gon - na
los - er, _____   read ___ it on the
los - er, _____   nev - er take it

fall _____ when you re - al - ize   you
wall _____ then re - al - ize   you
all _____ 'cause it's eas - i - er   and

To Coda

just can't have it all? _____
just don't need it all, ___
fast - er when you fall. ___

hey, you just don't need it

Bridge

all. _____ You don't need it all. _____

He'll nev - er make an - y en - e - mies, en - e - mies.

7

He won't com-plain if he's caught on his knees. _____

He'll al-ways ask, he'll al-ways say please. _____

D.C. al Coda

Coda

_____ Ah, you just don't need it all, _____

you just don't need it all.

Fire Lake

Words and Music by Bob Seger

* *Originally recorded in A major.*

Who wants to break the news a-bout Un-cle

Joe? You re-mem-ber

Un-cle Joe. ___ He was the one a-fraid to cut the cake. _____

Who wants to

tell poor Aunt ___ Sar - ah

Joe's run off _____ to Fire ___ Lake? _____

Joe's run off _____ to Fire _____ Lake. _

Bridge

_____ Who wants to brave those

bronze beau - ties, ly - in' in the

sun with their long, soft hair fall -

- in', fly - in' as they

run? Oh, they smile so shy and they

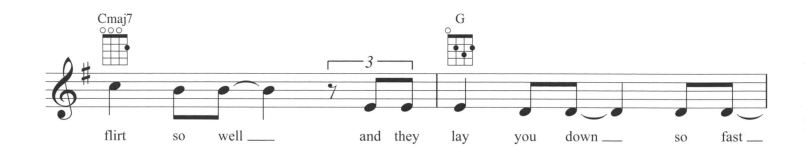

flirt so well ____ and they lay you down ____ so fast ____

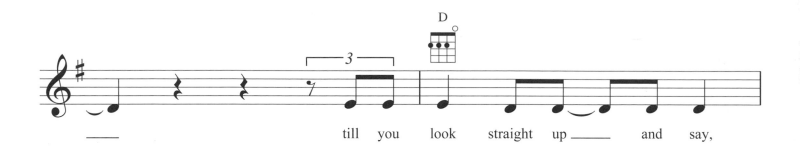

____ till you look straight up ____ and say,

"Oh Lord, am I real - ly here at last?"

Verse

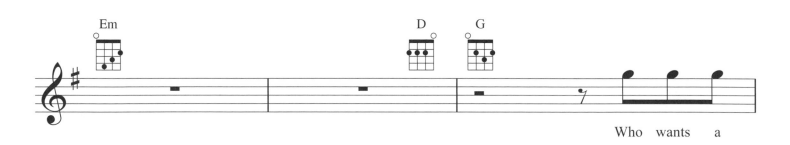

2. Who wants to play those eights _ and ac - es?

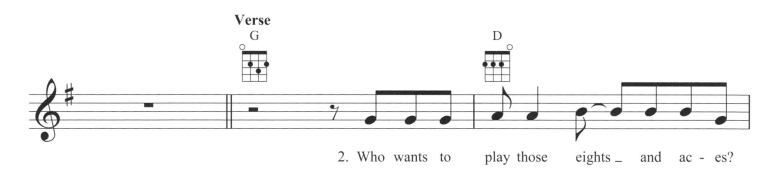

Who wants a

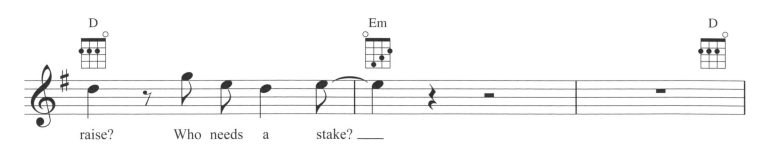

raise? Who needs a stake? ____

Who wants to take that long shot gam - ble

and head out _____ to Fire ___ Lake? __

Outro

_____ (Who wants to

go to Fire Lake?) _____

1.

(Who wants to go to Fire _____ Lake?) __

2.

___

Betty Lou's Gettin' Out Tonight

Words and Music by Bob Seger

First note

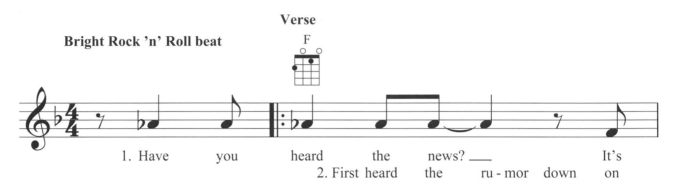

Bright Rock 'n' Roll beat

Verse

1. Have you heard the news? ___ It's
2. First heard the ru-mor down on

all o-ver town. ___ If you ain't heard it, boys, you
Twelfth ___ and Main. ___ The poor ___ drug-gist, he was

bet-ter sit down. I got the sto-ry here. It's hot off the press. ___
go-in' in-sane. His stuff is sell-ing out like nev-er be-fore. ___

Brace your-self, now, and take a deep breath. Grab a hold of some-thing.
He fi-n'lly had to up and close ___ the store. All the boys were get-tin'

Hold on tight. ___ Bet-ty Lou's _ get-tin' out ___ to-night. ___
read-y to fight. ___ Bet-ty Lou's ___ get-tin' out ___ to-night. ___

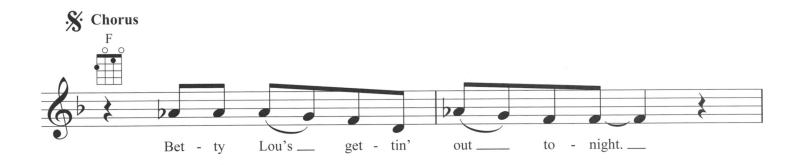

Bet - ty   Lou's ___ get - tin'   out ___   to - night. ___

Bet - ty   Lou's ___ get - tin'   out ___   to - night. ___

She   was   bad.   Her   mom - ma   got   mad.

But   now   her   mom - ma   says   it's   all ___   right. ___

All   the   boys   are   get - tin'   read - y   and   right. ___

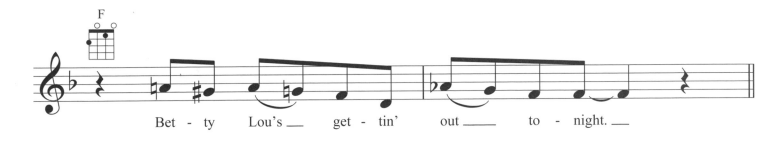

Bet - ty   Lou's ___ get - tin'   out ___   to - night. ___

Bridge

(Instrumental)　　　　　　　　　Bet-ty Lou.　　　　　　　　　　　　Bet-ty Lou.

To Coda

{ It's all true.　　　　　　　　　　　　　　　　　It's real-ly true. }
{ Yes, it's true.　　　　　　　　　　　　　　　　Bet-ty Lou. }

D.S. al Coda

(Spoken:) What do you think about that, boys?

Coda

Well, ___

Outro-Chorus

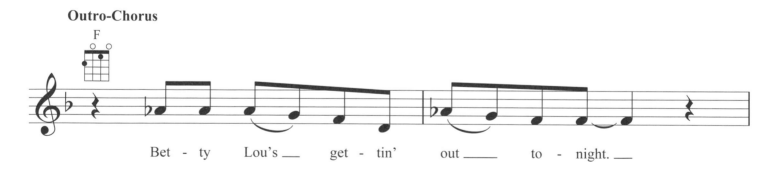

Bet - ty　Lou's ___　get - tin'　out ___　to - night. ___

Bet - ty　Lou's ___　get - tin'　out ___　to - night. ___

She was bad. Her mom-ma got mad. But now her mom-ma says

it's all ___ right. ___ All the boys are get - tin' read - y and right. ___

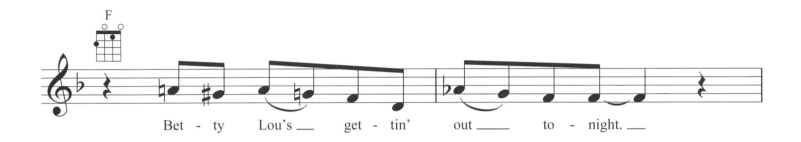

Bet - ty Lou's ___ get - tin' out ___ to - night. ___

Her mom - ma said that it would be all right. ___

Bet - ty Lou's ___ get - tin' out ___ to - night. ___ Grab a hold of some-thing.

Hold on tight. ___ Bet - ty Lou's get - tin' out ___ to - night. ___

Feel Like a Number

Words and Music by Bob Seger

Originally recorded in E major.

I work my back ___ till it's wracked ___
To teach - ers, I'm ___ just an - oth -

___ with pain. ___ The boss can't e - ven re - call ___ my name. ___ I
- er child. _ To I. R. S., ___ I'm an - oth - er file. ___ I'm

show up late ___ and I'm docked; ___ it nev - er fails.
just an - oth - er con - sen - sus on ___ the street.

𝄋 Pre-Chorus

I (1.) feel like just an - oth - er
(2., 3.) Gon - na cruise out of this cit - y;

spoke in a great ___ big wheel, ___ like a
head ___ down to ___ the sea. ___ Gon - na

ti - ny blade ___ of grass ___ in a great ___ big field. _
shout out at ___ the o - cean, "Hey ___ it's me!" _

Hollywood Nights

Words and Music by Bob Seger

First note

Verse
Moderately bright Rock beat

1. She stood there, bright as the sun, on that
3. He'd head - ed west 'cause he felt that a

Cal - i - for - nia coast.
change would do ___ him good.

He was a
See some old

Mid - west - ern boy on his own.
friends, good for the soul.

She looked at him with those soft eyes, so in - no - cent ___ and blue.
She had been born with a face that would let her get ___ her way.

He knew right then he was too far from
He saw that face and he lost all con -

Originally recorded in E major.

Verse

home.
trol.

hand and she led him a - long that gold - en beach.
night and day af - ter day it went on and on.

They watched the waves tum - ble o - ver the sand.
Then came that morn - ing he woke up a - lone.

2. She took his
4. Night af - ter

They drove for miles and miles ___ up those
He spent all night star - ing down at the

twist - ing, turn - ing roads.
lights of ___ L. A.,

High - er and
won - der - ing

high - er and high - er they climbed.
if he could ev - er go home.

And those Hol -
And those Hol -

§ **Chorus**

C ... F

- ly - wood nights   in those Hol - ly - wood hills:
- ly - wood nights   in those Hol - ly - wood hills:

C7sus4

she was look - ing so right   in her dia -
it was look - ing so right.   It was giv -

C

- monds and frills.   Oh, those big ____ cit - y nights __
- ing him chills.   Oh, those big ____ cit - y nights __

F

in those high, ____ roll - ing hills, ____   a -
in those high, ____ roll - ing hills, ____   a -

C7sus4   C   **1.**   *To Coda* ⊕

bove all the lights,   she had all ____ of her skills.
bove all the lights,   with a pas - sion that kills.

2.

D.S. al Coda
(Lyric 1)

And those Hol -

⊕ **Coda**

Mainstreet

Words and Music by Bob Seger

First note

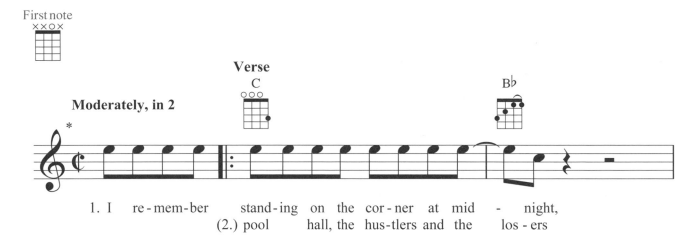

1. I re-mem-ber stand-ing on the cor-ner at mid - night,
(2.) pool hall, the hus-tlers and the los - ers

tryin' to get my cour-age up.
used to watch 'em through the glass.

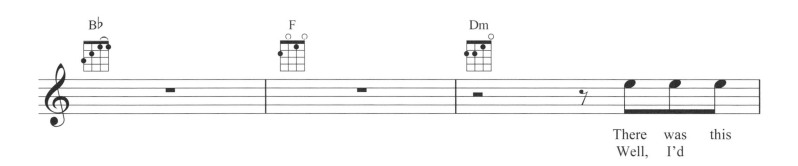

There was this
Well, I'd

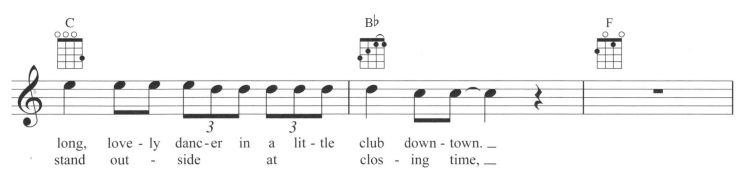

long, love - ly danc-er in a lit - tle club down - town. __
stand out - side at clos - ing time, __

Originally recorded in D major.

I loved to watch her do her stuff. __
just to watch her walk on past. __

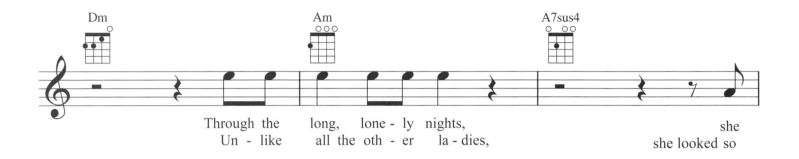

Through the long, lone - ly nights, she
Un - like all the oth - er la - dies, she looked so

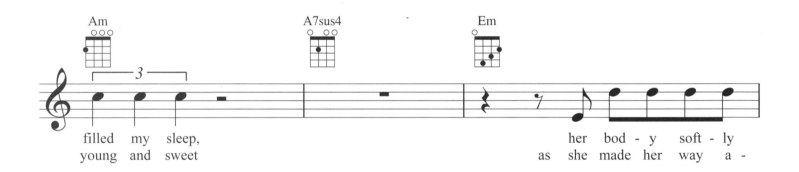

filled my sleep, her bod - y soft - ly
young and sweet as she made her way a -

sway - in' to that smok - y beat, down on
lone __ down that emp - ty street, down on

Chorus

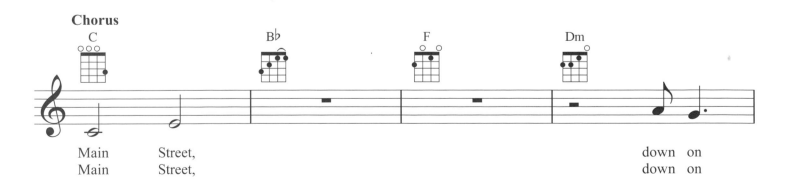

Main Street, down on
Main Street, down on

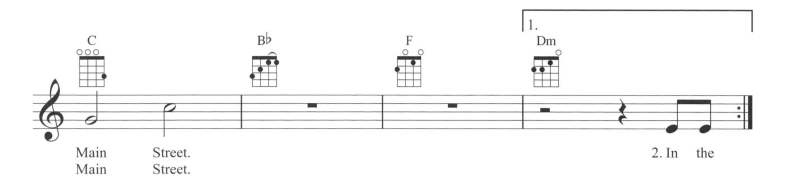

Main Street.
Main Street.

2. In the

Bridge

And some-times e - ven now, when I'm feel - in'

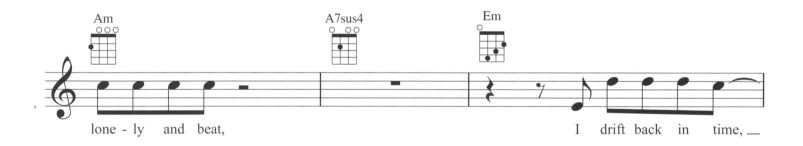

lone - ly and beat, I drift back in time, __

__ and I find ___ my feet down on

Outro-Chorus

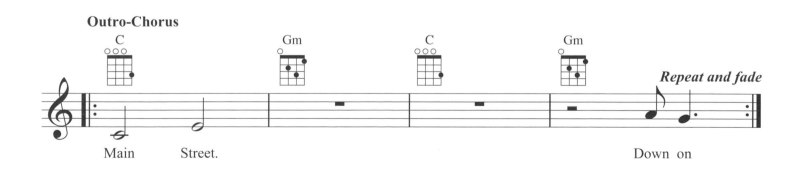

Repeat and fade

Main Street.

Down on

In Your Time

Words and Music by Bob Seger

1. In your time, the in-no-cence __ will fall __
(2.) waves will crash a-cross __ your south-
(3.) all the dead ends and __ the les-

__ a-way.
-ern capes.
-sons learned,

In your time, the
Mas-sive storms will
af-ter all the

mis-sion bells __ will toll, __
reach your east-ern shores. __
stars have turned __ to stone, __

oh. __

All a-long __
Fields of green __
there'll be peace __

the cor-ri-dors __ and riv-er-beds,
will tum-ble through __ your sum-mer days,
a-cross the great __ un-bro-ken void,

To Coda

there'll be signs in your __
by de-sign in your __
all be-nign in your __

Bridge

time. 2. Tow'r - ing time. Feel the

wind and set your - self ___ the bold - er course.

Keep your heart as o - pen as ___ a shrine; ___

___ you'll sail ___ the per - fect line. ___

D.S. al Coda Coda **Outro**

3. Af - ter time. You'll be fine ___

in your ___ time.

Like a Rock

Words and Music by Bob Seger

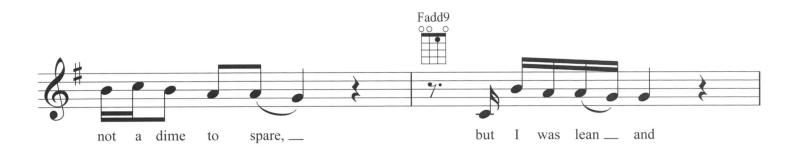

not a dime to spare, ___ but I was lean __ and

sol - id ev -'ry - where, _ like a rock.

Verse

3. My hands were stead - y, my eyes were clear and bright. _
5. *See additional lyrics*

My walk had pur - pose, my steps were quick and light, _

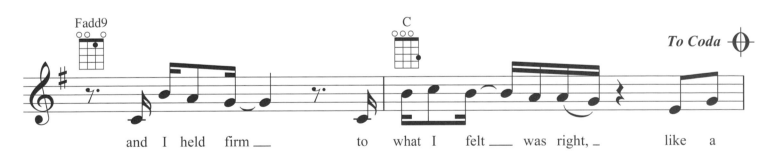

and I held firm __ to what I felt __ was right, _ like a

To Coda ⊕

Chorus

rock. Like a rock, I was

strong as I ___ could be; ___ like a rock, noth - in'

ev - er got ___ to me; ___ like a rock, I was

some - thin' to see, _ like a rock. And I

Bridge

stood _ ar-row straight, _ un - en - cum - bered by the weight _ of all ___ these

hus - tlers and ___ their schemes. _ I ___ stood proud, _

___ I stood tall, ___ high ___ a - bove it all. ___ I

Additional Lyrics

4. Twenty years now; where'd they go?
   Twenty years; I don't know.
   I sit and I wonder sometimes
   Where they've gone.

5. And sometimes late at night,
   When I'm bathed in the firelight,
   The moon comes callin' a ghostly white,
   And I recall.

Night Moves

Words and Music by Bob Seger

Out past the corn - fields where the woods __ got heav - y,

out in the back seat of my Six - ty Chev - y,

work - in' ___ on mys - t'ries with - out _____ an - y clues. _____

Chorus

Work - in' on our night moves, __

tryin' to make __ some front-page, drive-in news. __ Work - in' on our

night moves in the sum - mer - time, __

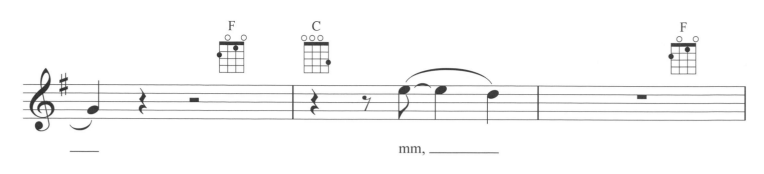

mm, _____

in the sweet ___ sum - mer - time. _____

Verse

2. We weren't in love.   Oh,   no, far from it.

We weren't search - in' for some pie - in - the - sky sum - mit.

We were just ___ young and ___ rest - less and bored, ___

liv - ing by the sword. _____

And we'd steal a - way ev - 'ry chance we could

to the back room, to the al - ley, or the trust - y woods. _____

I used her, she used me; ___ but nei - ther one cared. _____

Chorus

We were get - tin' our share, ___ work - in' on our night moves, _____

tryin' to lose ___ the awk - ward, teen - age blues, ___ work - in' on our

night moves. It was sum - mer - time, ___

37

mm, _____ sweet _

sum - mer - time, sum - mer - time. And

Bridge

oh, _____ the won - der. _____

We felt the light - ning. Yeah, _

and we wait - ed on the thun - der,

wait - ed on the thun - der. _____

I a-woke last night to the sound of thun-der.

How far off, I sat and won-dered.

Start-ed hum-ming a song __ from nine-teen six-ty-two. ____

Ain't it fun-ny how the night moves __

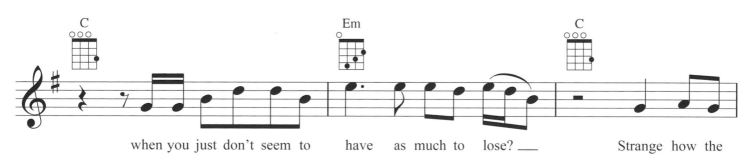

when you just don't seem to have as much to lose? __ Strange how the

night moves ____ with au-tumn clos-ing in. __

Old Time Rock & Roll

Words and Music by George Jackson and Thomas E. Jones III

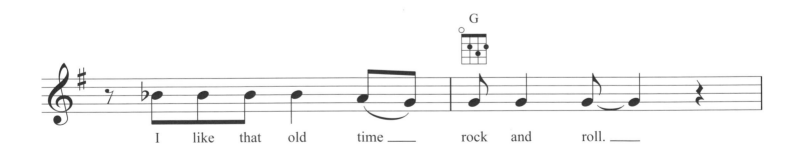

1. Just take those old rec-ords off the shelf. _ I'll sit and lis-ten to 'em

2. *Instrumental*

(3.) *See additional lyrics*

by my-self. _ To-day's mu-sic ain't got the same soul.

I like that old time _ rock and roll. _

Don't try to take me to a dis-co. You'll nev-er e-ven get me

out on the floor. ___ In ten min-utes I'll be late for the door. ___

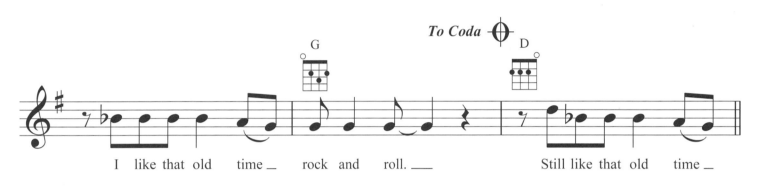

To Coda ⊕

I like that old time ___ rock and roll. ___ Still like that old time ___

Chorus

rock and roll. ___ That kind of mu-sic just soothes the soul. ___

I rem-i-nisce a-bout the days of old ___ with that old ___ time

1.

2.

D.S. al Coda

rock and roll. ___ 3. Won't go to hear 'em play a

Outro-Chorus

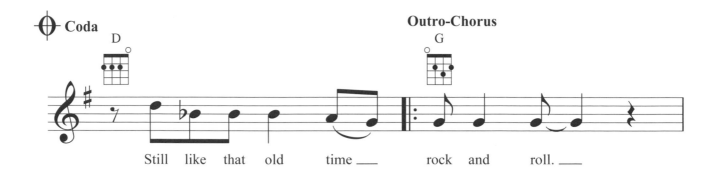

Still like that old time ___ rock and roll. ___

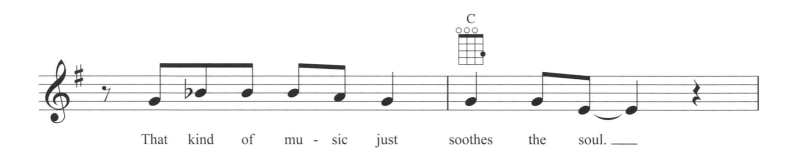

That kind of mu - sic just soothes the soul. ___

I rem - i - nisce a - bout the days of old ___

Repeat and fade

with that old _____ time rock and roll. ___ Still like that old time ___

Additional Lyrics

3. Won't go to hear 'em play a tango.
   I'd rather hear some blues or funky old soul.
   There's only one sure way to get me to go:
   Start playin' old time rock and roll.
   Call me a relic, call me what you will.
   Say I'm old-fashioned, say I'm over the hill.
   Today's music ain't got the same soul.
   I like that old time rock and roll.

Ramblin' Gamblin' Man

Words and Music by Bob Seger

* Originally recorded in E major.

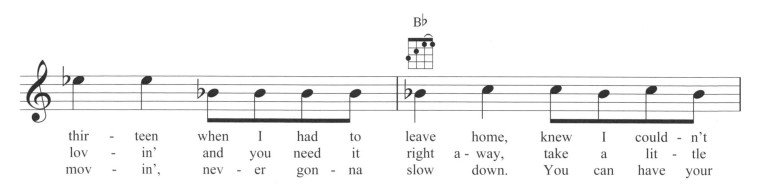

thir - teen when I had to leave home, knew I could - n't
lov - in' and you need it right a - way, take a lit - tle
mov - in', nev - er gon - na slow down. You can have your

1.

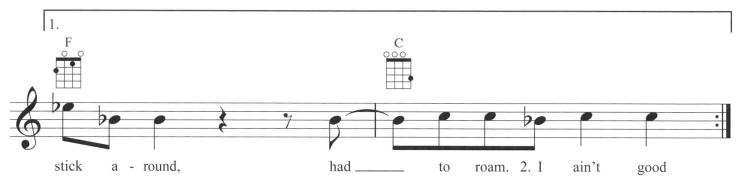

stick a - round, had _____ to roam. 2. I ain't good

2., 3.

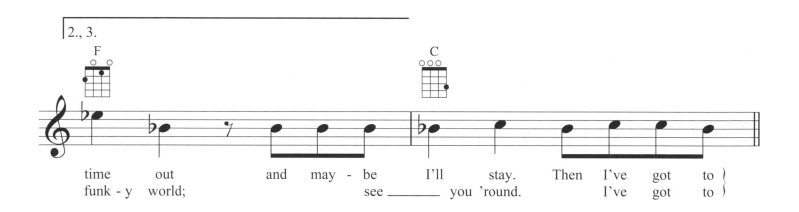

time out and may - be I'll stay. Then I've got to
funk - y world; see _____ you 'round. I've got to

Chorus

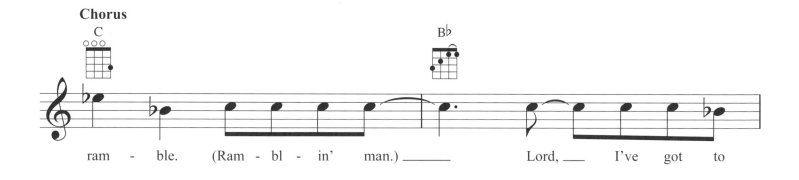

ram - ble. (Ram - bl - in' man.) _____ Lord, ___ I've got to

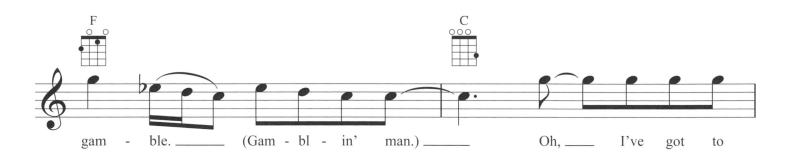

gam - ble. _____ (Gam - bl - in' man.) _____ Oh, ___ I've got to

44

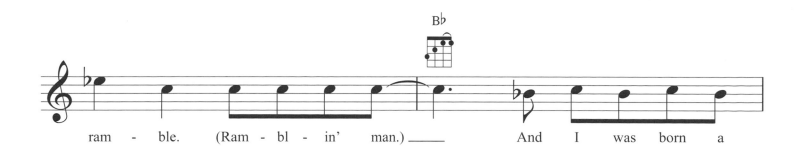

ram - ble. (Ram - bl - in' man.) _____ And I was born a

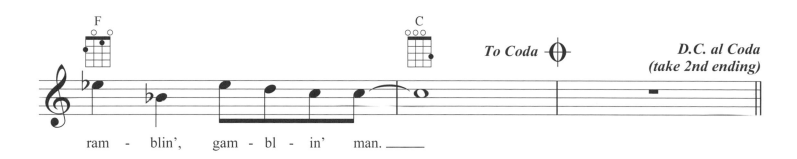

To Coda ⊕

D.C. al Coda
(take 2nd ending)

ram - blin', gam - bl - in' man. _____

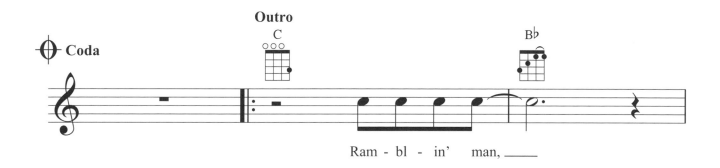

⊕ Coda

Outro

Ram - bl - in' man, _____

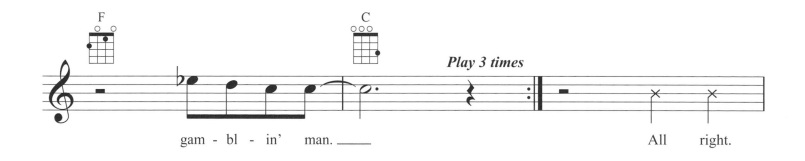

Play 3 times

gam - bl - in' man. _____ All right.

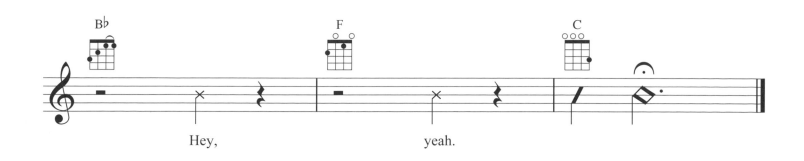

Hey, yeah.

The Real Love

Words and Music by Bob Seger

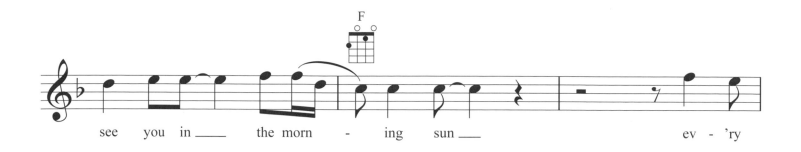

see you in ____ the morn - ing sun ____ ev - 'ry

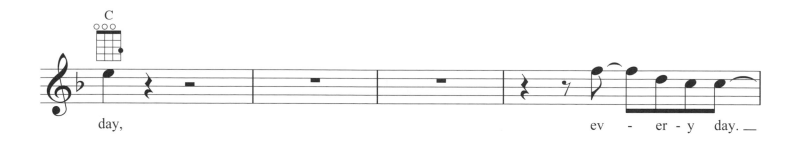

day,   ev - er - y day. ____

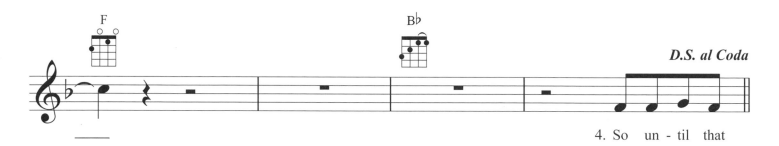

____   4. So un - til that

Coda

Real ____ love.

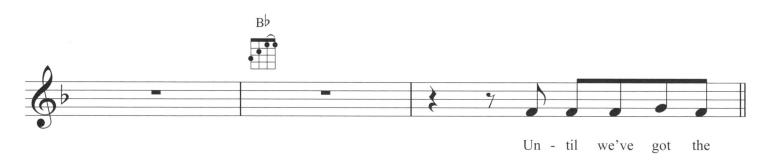

Un - til we've got the

Outro

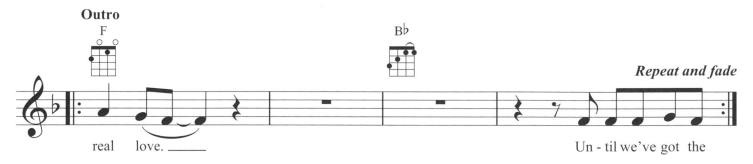

real love. ____   Un - til we've got the

Still the Same

Words and Music by Bob Seger

you were quick - er than they thought. _____
on - ly loss you could for - sake, _____ the
I just turned and walked a - way. _____

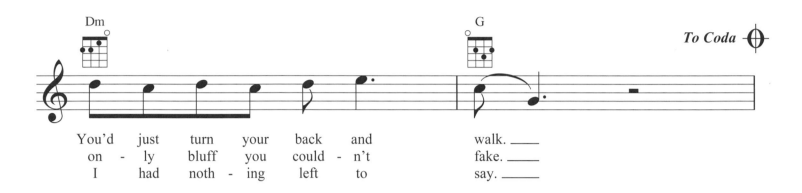

To Coda ⊕

You'd just turn your back and walk. _____
on - ly bluff you could - n't fake. _____
I had noth - ing left to say. _____

Chorus

1.

2.   C

2. You   And you're still the same. _____
                                                                                    I

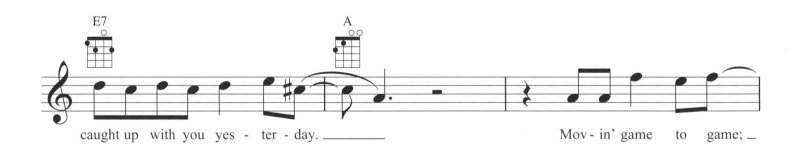

caught up with you yes - ter - day. _____   Mov - in' game to game; _____

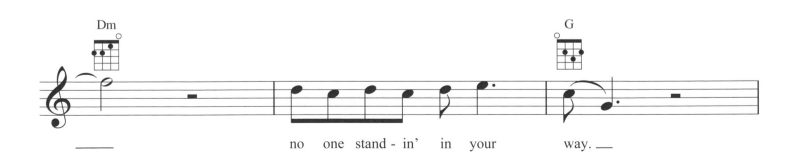

_____   no one stand - in' in your way. _____

50

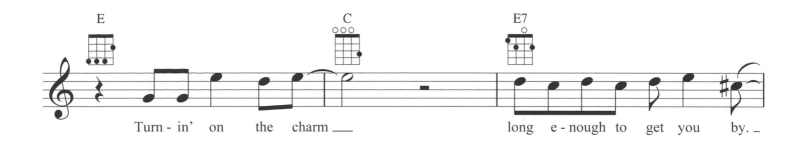

Turn - in' on the charm ___ long e - nough to get you by. _

___ ___ You're still the same. ___

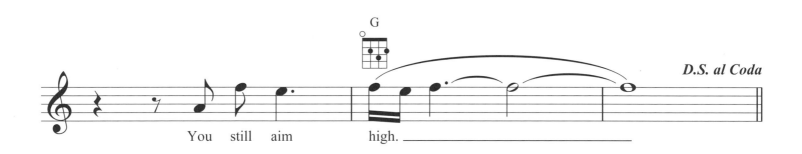

D.S. al Coda

You still aim high. _____

Outro-Chorus

Coda

'Cause you're still the same. _____
___
___
___
___

Repeat and fade

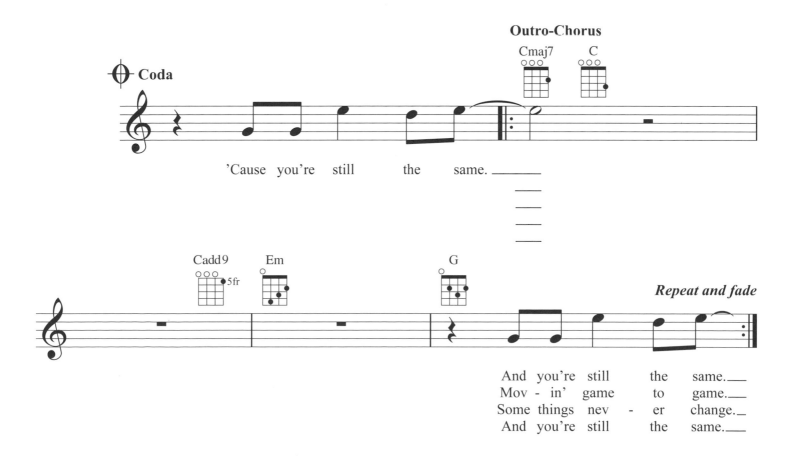

And you're still the same.___
Mov - in' game to game.___
Some things nev - er change._
And you're still the same.___

Roll Me Away

from the Touchstone Picture ARMAGEDDON
Words and Music by Bob Seger

1. Took a look down a west-bound road; __ right a - way __ __ I made my choice. __ Head-ed out to my big two - wheel - er; I was tired of my __ own voice. __ Took a bead on the north - ern plains __ and just rolled __ __ that pow - er on.

Verse
Moderately fast

C   Dm7

2. Twelve hours out of Mack-i-naw Cit - y, ___ stopped in a bar ___
3. Stood a-lone on a moun - tain - top, _____ star - in' out ___

C   F   C

___ to have a brew. ___   Met a girl and we
___ at the Great Di - vide.   I could go east,

Dm7   C

had a few drinks, _ and I told _____ her what I'd de - cid - ed to do. ___
I could go west; ___ it was all _____ up to _____ me to de - cide. ___

F   G

___   She looked _ out the win-dow a long, ___
___   Just then ___ I saw a young _

C   F   C

___ long mo - ment, then she looked in - to my eyes. ___
___ hawk fly - in' and my soul be - gan to rise. ___

G

She did-n't have to say a thing.
And pret - ty soon   I

Chorus

knew what she was think - in':
my heart was sing - in':

Roll, _____ roll me a-way. Won't you
Roll, _____ roll me a-way, I'm gon - na

roll me a - way __ to - night.
roll me a - way __ to - night.

I too am lost; I
Got - ta keep roll - in',

feel dou - ble - crossed, __ and I'm
got - ta keep rid - in', keep

sick of what's wrong __ and what's
search - in' till I _____ find what's

right. _
right. _

We nev - er e - ven said a word; we just walked out __
And as the sun - set fad - ed, I spoke to the faint -

To Coda

____ and got on that bike.
- est first star - light.

And we rolled, _

and we rolled __ clean out of sight.

54

Till It Shines

Words and Music by Bob Seger

First note

Verse
Moderately

1. Take a - way my ___ in - hi - bi - tion,
2. Like an ech - o ___ down a can - yon,

take a - way my ___ sol - i - tude.
nev - er com - ing ___ back as clear,

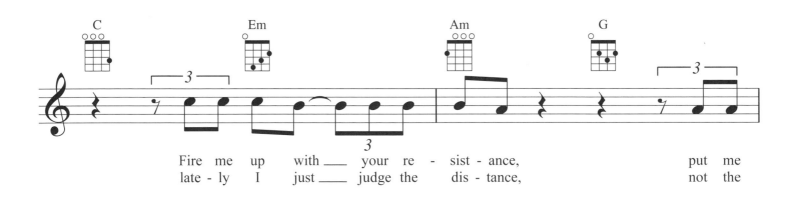

Fire me up with ___ your re - sist - ance,
late - ly I just ___ judge the dis - tance,

put me
not the

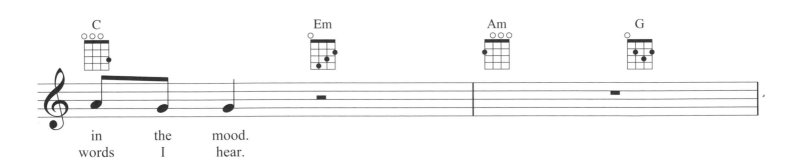

in the mood.
words I hear.

Storm the walls a - round this pris - on.
I've been too long on these is - lands.
3. Instrumental

Leave the in - mates, ___ free the guards.
I've been far too ___ long a - lone.

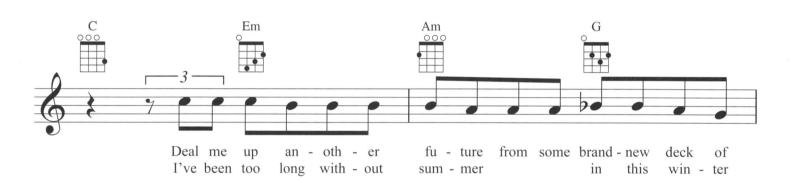

Deal me up an - oth - er fu - ture from some brand - new deck of
I've been too long with - out sum - mer in this win - ter

Chorus

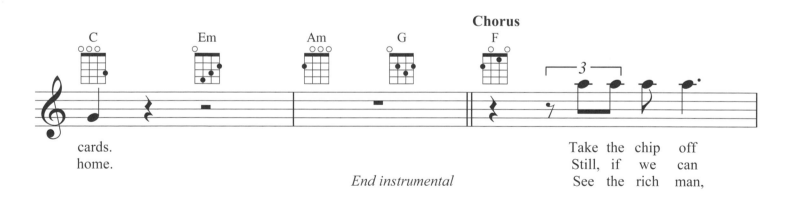

cards.
home.   Take the chip off
End instrumental   Still, if we can
                                            See the rich man,

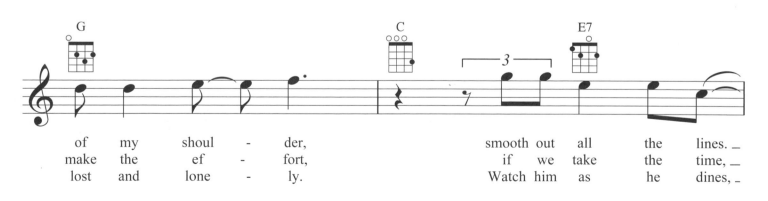

of   my   shoul - der,   smooth out all   the   lines. _
make   the   ef -   fort,   if   we   take   the   time, _
lost   and   lone - ly.   Watch him as   he   dines, _

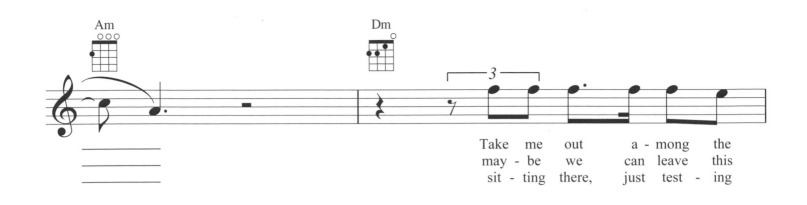

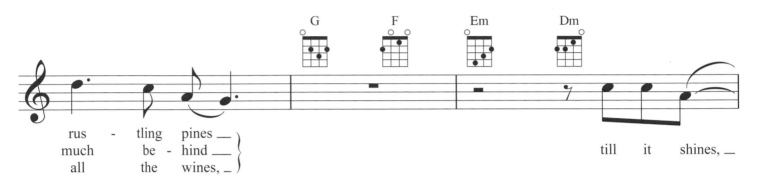

Take me out a - mong the
may - be we can leave this
sit - ting there, just test - ing

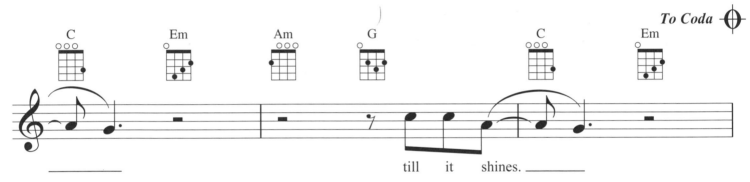

rus - tling pines __
much be - hind __
all the wines, __

till it shines, __

To Coda

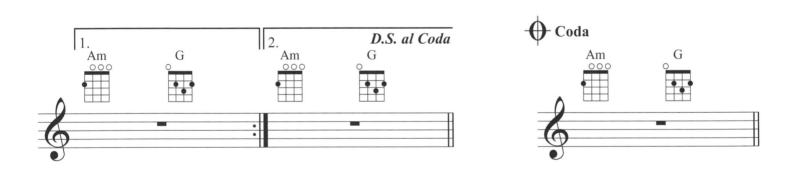

till it shines. _____

1.

2. *D.S. al Coda*

Coda

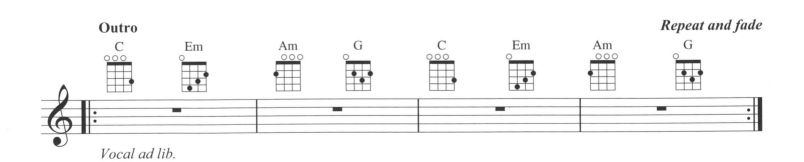

Outro   *Repeat and fade*

Vocal ad lib.

Turn the Page

Words and Music by Bob Seger

But your thoughts will soon be wan-der-in', ___ the

way they al - ways do, ___ when you're rid - in' six - teen hours ___ and there's

noth-in' much ___ to do. ___ And you don't feel much like rid - in'; you just

wish the trip ___ was through. _____

𝄋 **Chorus**

Say, here I am on the

road a - gain. ___ There I am, up on the

Additional Lyrics

2. Well, you walk into a restaurant strung out from the road,
And you feel the eyes upon you as you're shakin' off the cold;
You pretend it doesn't bother you but you just want to explode.
Most times you can't hear 'em talk, other times you can,
All the same old cliches, "Is that a woman or a man?"
And you always seem outnumbered, you don't dare make a stand.

3. Out there in the spotlight you're a million miles away.
Every ounce of energy you try to give away
As the sweat pours out your body like the music that you play.
Later in the evening as you lie awake in bed
With the echoes from the amplifiers ringing in your head,
You smoke the day's last cigarette, remembering what she said.

Wait for Me

Words and Music by Bob Seger

You'll Accomp'ny Me

Words and Music by Bob Seger

Originally recorded in E major.

I've seen you smiling in the sum - mer sun.
I'll take my chanc - es, babe. I'll risk it all.

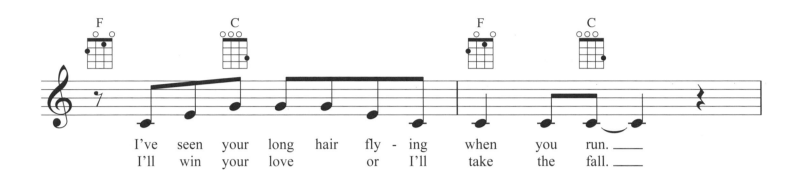

I've seen your long hair fly - ing when you run. ____
I'll win your love or I'll when take the fall. ____

I've made my mind up that it's meant to be.
I've made my mind up, girl. It's meant to be.

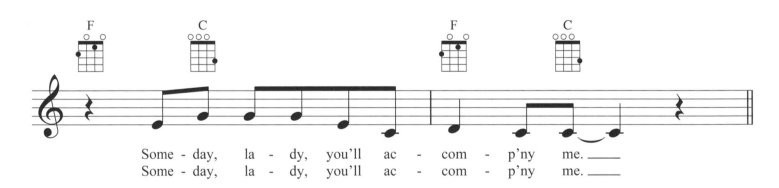

Some - day, la - dy, you'll ac - com - p'ny me. ____
Some - day, la - dy, you'll ac - com - p'ny me. ____

𝄋 Chorus

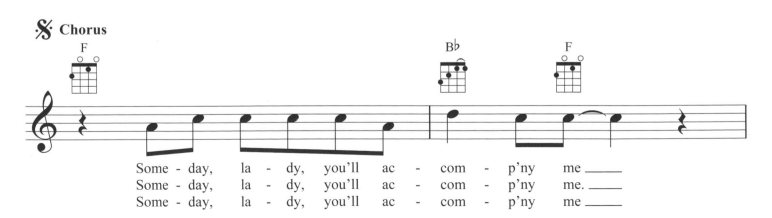

Some - day, la - dy, you'll ac - com - p'ny me ____
Some - day, la - dy, you'll ac - com - p'ny me. ____
Some - day, la - dy, you'll ac - com - p'ny me ____

out where the riv - ers meet the sound - ing sea. ____
It's writ - ten down some - where. It's got ____ to be. ____
out where the riv - ers meet the sound - ing sea. ____

You're high a - bove me now. You're wild and free. ____ Ah, but
You're high a - bove me, fly - ing wild and free. ____ Oh, but
I feel it in my soul. It's meant to be. ____ Oh,

some - day, la - dy, you'll ac - com - p'ny me. ____
some - day, la - dy, you'll ac - com - p'ny me. ____
some - day, la - dy, you'll ac - com - p'ny me. ____

To Coda

1.

Some - day, la - dy, you'll ac - com - p'ny me. ____
Some - day, la - dy, you'll ac -
Some - day, la - dy, you'll ac -

2.

D.S. al Coda

com - p'ny me. ____

Coda

com - p'ny me. ____

We've Got Tonight

Words and Music by Bob Seger

Originally recorded in B major.

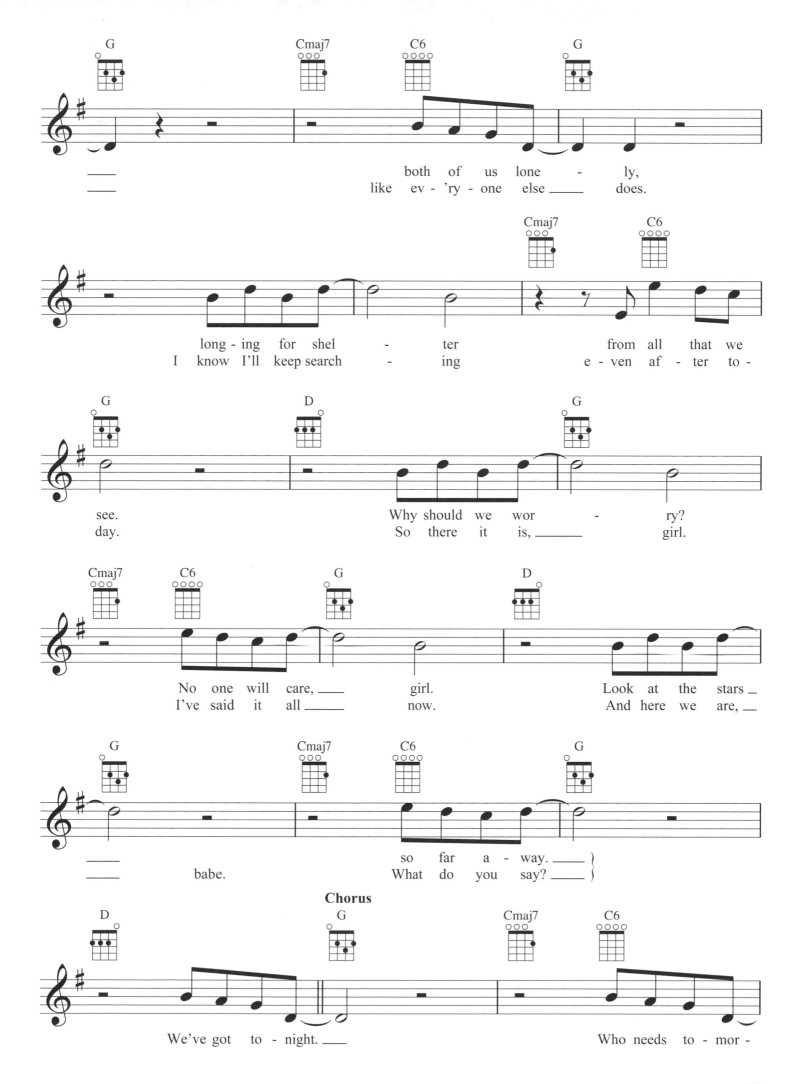

both of us lone - ly,
like ev - 'ry - one else ___ does.

long - ing for shel - ter from all that we
I know I'll keep search - ing e - ven af - ter to -

see.
day.

Why should we wor - ry?
So there it is, ___ girl.

No one will care, ___ girl.
I've said it all ___ now.

Look at the stars ___
And here we are, ___

babe.
so far a - way. ___)
What do you say? ___)

Chorus

We've got to - night. ___ Who needs to - mor -

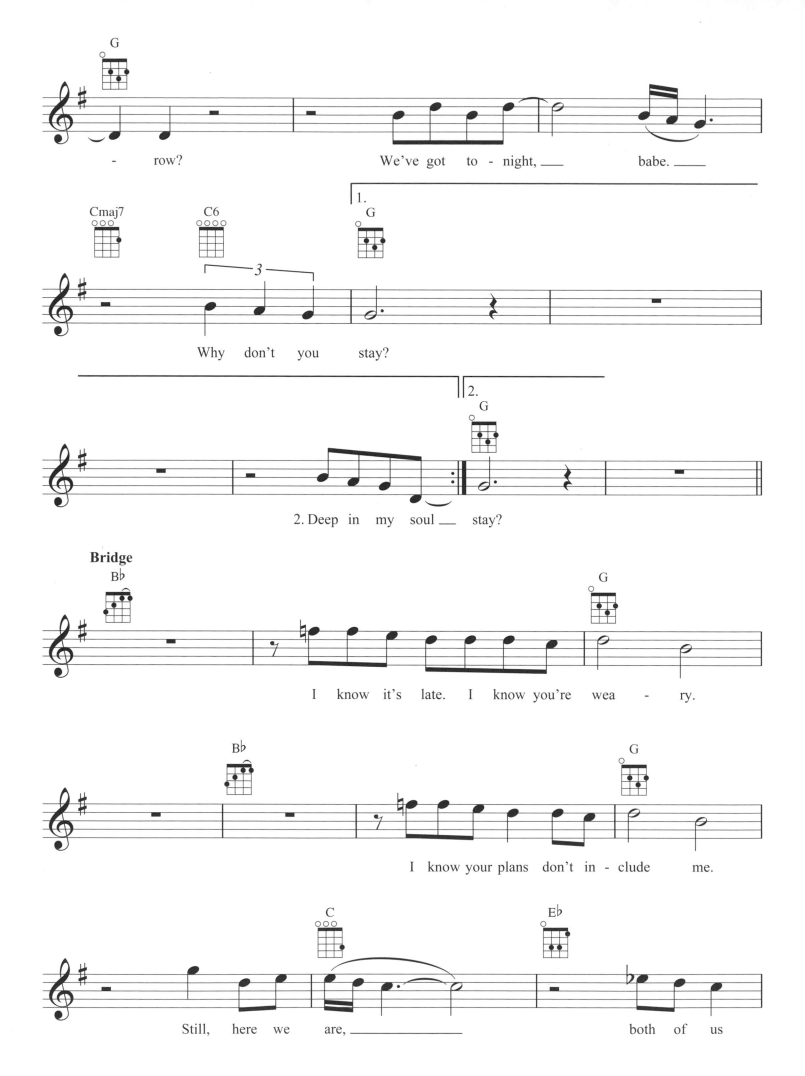

-row? We've got to - night, ____ babe. ____

Why don't you stay?

2. Deep in my soul ____ stay?

Bridge

I know it's late. I know you're wea - ry.

I know your plans don't in - clude me.

Still, here we are, ____ both of us

Chorus

Who needs to-mor - row? Let's make it last.

Let's find a way. _____ Turn out the light. _____

Come, take my hand now. We've got to-night, _____

_____ babe. Why don't you stay? 4. Oh, _____ we've got to-night. _____

Coda

stay? _____

Outro

Oh. _____

_____ Oh, why don't you stay?